A Middle School
Survival Guide

A Middle School
Survival Guide

Written by: Annie Dunford   Illustrated by: Lindsay Ford

Copyright© 2019. All rights reserved. No part of this book may be reproduced in any form or by any electronic or mechanical means, including information storage and retrieval systems, without permission in writing from the author; except by a reviewer, who may quote brief passages in a review.

Published and printed in the United States of America.

First Edition

Dunford, Annie
A Middle School Survival Guide/Annie Dunford
Just The Box®, www.JustTheBox.com
ISBN: 978-1-948-60429-1

Library of Congress Control Number: 2019937437

Illustrations & Layout: Lindsay Ford
Prepared for publication by Write|Publish|Sell

Printed by Lightning Source, Inc

For my sister, Abby Dunford.

Also... to every student, cohort, classmate, friend, teacher, parent that has helped a student along the way.

Dedicated to my little sister, who will follow me into middle school. May this help you, dear Abby, and may you learn from my experiences. My words of wisdom come from a writing assignment I was given on "What Peace On Earth Means to Me" – and the turmoil of middle school, which rattled me.

We can make peace on earth by making the right decisions, such as following the rules and the little voice in your head that tells you to do the right things.

We need to recycle on the Earth and preserve it for years to come. The Earth is not like a fire. If our house catches on fire, we can move to a new one, but there is only one planet for us. We can't move to Mars. It is vital that we use our brains and help protect the Earth - not destroy it.

We can't forget about the plants and animals either - because without them we wouldn't be alive.

Also, make peace by paying attention to your surroundings, such as stoplights, other people, and obstacles.

Life on Earth is a gift...so let's pursue it.

Table of Contents

Maps — p. 11
How to never look like a sixth grader
- Upstairs Map — p. 18
- Downstairs Map — p. 19

Hallways — p. 21
You are now a minotaur trapped in the labyrinth of school hallways.

Groups, peers, cohorts... — p. 29
Lions and tigers and bears, oh my!

Teachers... — p. 53
aka the gatekeepers

Maps

How to never look like a sixth grader

Rule #1.

Always know where you are going.

Know this--seventh and eighth graders can always tell the rookies, commonly known as sixth graders, in middle school. How? They are as lost as last year's Thanksgiving turkey. So how do you not look like a lost sixth grader? Easy, you memorize the school map and know your way around before you arrive on day one of class. Why? 'Cause it's a jungle out there. Others have made it...so will you. As they say in the Hunger Games, may the odds be ever in your favor.

If you learn the key places you have to be, you will also know the key points others will need to find (cafeteria, bathroom, front office). Soon you will be the "Goddess or God of Knowledge and Directions." Other mere mortal sixth graders will bow down before you to seek your knowledge...and the day an upper classman comes to "sharpshoot" you with questions, AND you can actually answer, your status of having supreme knowledge of the "lay of the land" will be validated. That's right, cowhands.... There's a new sheriff in town and she's a sixth grader!

So your mission, should you choose to accept it, is to memorize your school hallways and classrooms. Day one, when you enter, walk with confidence that YOU DO KNOW where you are GOING and it is to the TOP!

P.S. If you have an older sibling, ask him or her to sketch a map for you. Your life will be so much easier!

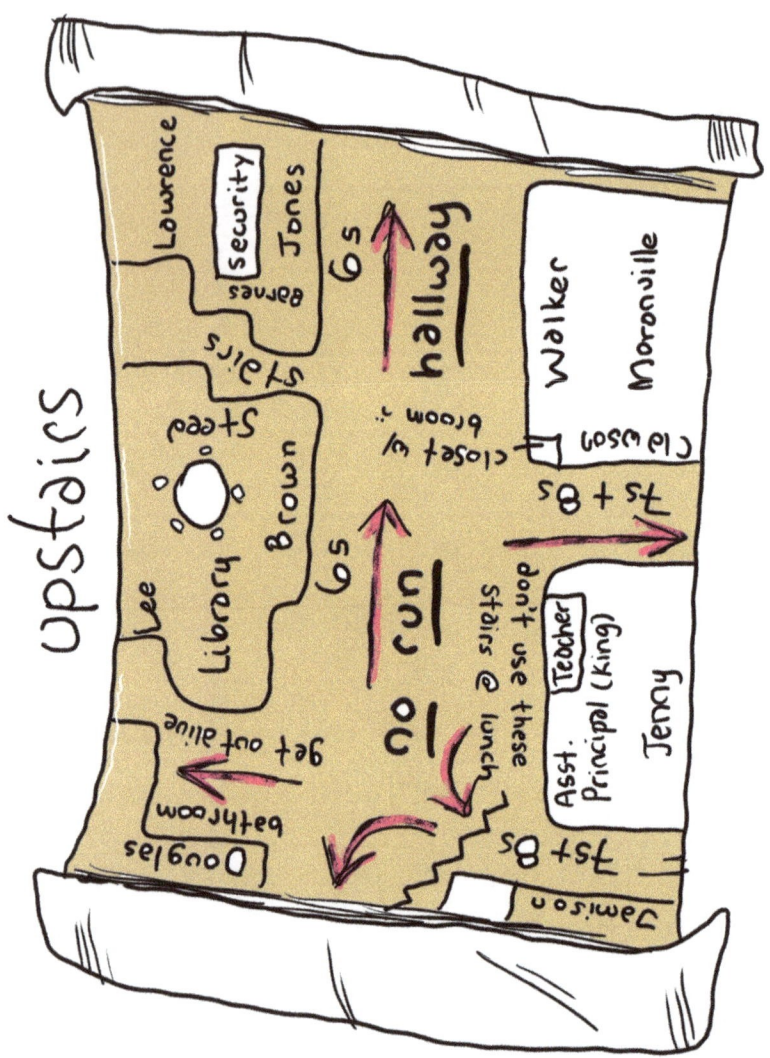

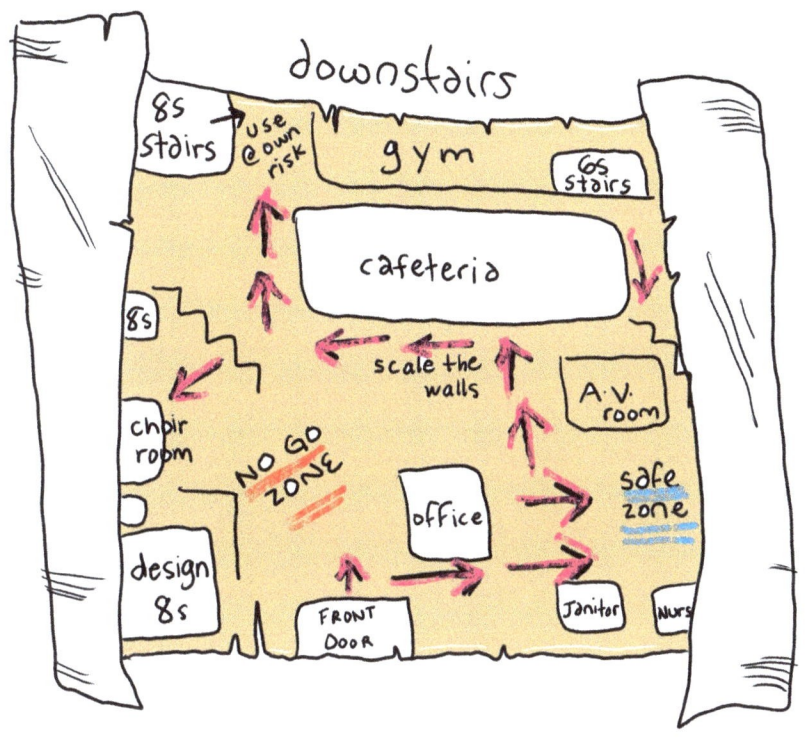

Here's a sample school map I wish I'd had on day one of sixth grade. I was lost. Fortunately, teachers understand and are patient. They give students a week or two to learn their way about.

Hallways

you are now a minotaur trapped in the labyrinth of school hallways.

Oh, how you will long for the days of orderly movement down the hallway by class, single file with your hands to your side...everyone moving ever so quietly in unison or holding hands to keep from getting lost.

before

after

NO MORE! Welcome to the Thunderdome of Middle School, where chaos reigns and noise levels rise from the depths like the Phoenix from the ashes!

School hallways are the equivalent of interstate highways, but, in lieu of cars, everyone walks. And just like cars on the highway, some students move with purpose, some move to be seen, and some don't move at all. There are "speed traps" or areas to avoid and often traffic jams.

Hallways are always very crowded, especially in the beginning of the school year. Those sixth graders who did not heed my counsel in the earlier chapter to learn the school layout beforehand are especially apt to clog the halls. They are the poor lost souls trying to walk up the stairwell that is for one-way traffic coming down.

you will also find that the hallways, for some reason, are always more crowded around some teachers' areas than others. I have yet to figure out why, unless it is because everyone is avoiding those other teachers' "hallway" space for fear of retribution and being called out as if in the Hunger Games™.

Lunch is H-E-C-T-I-C. Again, no more moving to lunch in an orderly manner. you are out of class and to the locker first, only moving directly to the lunchroom if you have squeezed your lunch into your book bag. you will now experience the fastest 20 minutes of your life...so get your lunch and go, ASAP!

In the hallways, you will find that the "upper classmen," aka seventh and eighth graders, are very mean to sixth graders. For some reason, they forget they were all in the same grade school just a few years ago. Suddenly, they are the czars of the planet and cannot associate with naives who sit in the pit of the Globe Theatre watching the play of life before us.

Groups, peers, cohorts...

Lions and tigers and bears, oh my!

While you had friends in elementary school, you will now be in classes with different peers, friends, and cohorts. No longer are you with the same group for the entire school day. The bonus is that you will have an opportunity to make great new friends. The unfortunate part is that the close, tight bonds of old friendships are loosened some as you are not with that same group everyday. But I prefer the positives--you will meet new people and make new friends.

By now, we are all starting to form our individual personas. We all know there is a class clown, but here are a few classifications my friends and I have observed and you might encounter as well. Is one more right than the other? No. The point is, we begin to form into groups, clusters, or--in terms of biology, which you will soon be taking-- "cells." We begin to form the cells that make up the organism.

Nerds

They think they know everything,
They always wanna talk to the
teacher and teach the class.

Plastics

These bratty girls think they have breasts and a butt...and they don't! They think they are better than anyone else. Very cliquey!

JOCKS

They are simply mean to be "cool." Most are cute but AWKWARD!

Greasies

They don't wash their hair or bathe.
Yuck, that is just gross.

Animos

They watch cartoons and are like Greasies but worse.

Cussers

These folks cuss like sailors and don't care--purely potty mouths.

Troublemakers

They talk back, act mean, and often have poor grades.

Flowers

They are nice, funny, and usually don't care what people think.

Bashfuls

REALLY shy! And they don't like social conflict.

So that sums up my assessment. You will form your own, but at least you know some of the personalities you will find yourself dealing with. From what I hear from freshmen returning from college, it doesn't change much when you get to college. It takes all kinds of kinds, as the song lyrics say.

Teachers...aka
the gatekeepers

Gone are the days when you have the one teacher for eight hours of your life. This is great when you have a great, fun, show-me-the-world kind of teacher, but it can be the equivalent of Chinese water torture if you don't. We will all have both--and everything in between--in our educational travels, and it starts with middle school.

Teachers, like students, will come in all shapes, sizes, intellects, and levels of passion. And don't think it is always the "new" teacher straight out of college who will have the greatest passion. Teachers who have forgotten more than we may ever learn can be wonderful. So here are categories that I have found teachers fall into:

Czar

They are all about their subject and do not talk, live, or breathe anything other than school. They often will "lose it" if you are late for class.

Czar Lite

These teachers are hard but fair and can even be nice, once you know the rules and play by them. Just don't get on their "bad side."

Favorites

These teachers will reveal they have a favorite--either one gender or a particular student or group of students.

ugly

They are just plain old mean. You will hear about these teachers the summer prior to starting sixth grade. I think if these people won the lottery, they would complain they had to go downtown to pickup the check.

Dentals

These teachers will banish you to the ends of the earth if you are caught chewing gum in their class. I only wish I knew why they have such a distaste for gum.

Analytics

These are your math teachers. And while they have been doing math for years, few can teach it. They too often forget we are just learning the stuff. I discovered "Why?" was the most complex question you can ask a math teacher. Some of them are great and you will hear about them (like the uglies but in a good way) before you ever start sixth grade. Get these teachers, if at all possible. It will make Algebra and Geometry so much easier to understand.

Intolerants

These teachers do not like "dumb" or "ignorant" students, whether they call them that or not. Why they became teachers in the first place is beyond me.

Screamers

These teachers are the loud ones. You will hear them when you are in other classes. Amazing that we are "counseled" for being loud, but I am not certain if a teacher ever faces the same fate.

<u>In Summary...</u>
<u>I was as scared as a long-tailed cat in a room full of</u>
<u>rocking chairs when I arrived for the sixth grade.</u>
<u>Middle school is prep school for high school, for</u>
<u>college, for life. We have to learn to work with all</u>
<u>types of people, personalities, and circumstances. As</u>
<u>my dad said, "You are not the first, and you won't</u>
<u>be the last. Walk straight, stand for what is right,</u>
<u>and everything else will take care of itself. And</u>
<u>remember, failure is not an option." I made it...you</u>
<u>will, too.</u>

www.ingramcontent.com/pod-product-compliance
Lightning Source LLC
Chambersburg PA
CBHW041319110526
44591CB00021B/2847